CW00819141

Mill Girls

POETS

Mo Blake
Kathryn Daly
Gwen McKerrell
Tracy Patrick

With Anna MacDonald

Published by Weaving Musical Threads 2013

The copyright for all poems and song lyrics remains with the authors © 2013. The authors have asserted their right under the Copyright, Designs and Patents Act 1988.

Legal Notice
All rights reserved. No part of this book may be reproduced, stored in a retrieval system, or transmitted in any form or by any means; electronic, mechanical, photocopying, recording or otherwise, without prior permission from the copyright holders. It should not be circulated without the publishers consent in any form of binding or cover other than that in which it is published.

First published 2013 by:
Weaving Musical Threads
Elise Kelly
Chairperson
14 Fife Avenue
Glasgow G52 3EW
www.weavingmusicalthreads.com
In association with Read Raw Press

Typesetting by Wullie Purcell
Internal design by Wullie Purcell and Caroline Watson
Cover design by Caroline Watson

Printed and bound by:
Bell & Bain
303 Burnfield Road
Thornliebank
Glasgow G46 7UQ

ISBN No   978-1-907000-13-3

Supported by Local Area Committees of Renfrewshire.

Dedicated to the mill workers and in special memory of
Ellen Farmer MBE (1938-2013) and Eleanor McAlpine (1937-2013)

Photos courtesy of the Paisley Daily Express

Foreword

Weaving Musical Threads (WMT) began with an arts festival to celebrate the cultural life of Renfrewshire as part of Music Nation and the Cultural Olympiad 2012. It was a weekend of inspiration and an opportunity for collaboration. Events took place throughout the region, bringing together art, music, dance, voice, literature, drama, film and history; a chance to celebrate where we live – the people, our history and place in the world.

A group of writers from Renfrewshire, intrigued by the industrial and social history of the area, created and performed poems in the Paisley Thread Mill Museum where the stories of the thread mills are found in photographs, memorabilia and conversations of the men and women who had worked there. The toil and pride of their labour and the hardships and pleasures of their lives inspired the poets and the formation of the *Mill Girls*: Tracy Patrick, Gwen McKerrell, Kathryn Daly and Mo Blake.

Paisley has an international reputation for its history as a textile town that began with the weavers and internationally known Paisley Pattern. At the turn of the 18th century a weaver, Peter Clark, began to experiment with cotton until he could produce a fine thread that was smooth and strong like silk. By 1810 the Clark family became the first cotton thread manufacturer in Paisley. Sixteen years later the Coats family also set up a thread mill. These two families would expand, develop and merge into an international thread manufacturing business that stills exists today. For nearly two centuries it employed thousands of workers in Paisley until the last mill closed in 1993. The contribution of these families to Paisley is still visible in the great historic buildings and statues that is their legacy. However, the labour of many provided the wealth. The immense contribution of the mill workers is found in the local museums, Paisley Thread Mill Museum and Sma' Shot Cottages, established and run by volunteers who understand the need to keep their stories alive. They preserve the details of ordinary lives and the radicalism that improved working conditions, colouring the history of a working town.

The *Mill Girls* retell these stories in their poems, remembering and celebrating the lives of the workers; the making of a place and its people that heartens the lives and spirit of contemporary women and men. Like many towns the decline in manufacturing has impacted negatively on the area for many decades. We are embracing the chance for heritage to revitalise the local economy and to rekindle pride, investment and interest.

The Mill Girls is a wonderful project of creativity and collaboration and one of which WMT is proud to be a part. It started with an arts festival, inspired locally and has become the dramatisation "Mill Girls on Tour" that is being performed in locations across Scotland. Joining the poets is musician and singer songwriter, Anna McDonald, whose lyrics for *Mill Girls Song*, commissioned by WMT, are included in this anthology.

These poems are expressive and descriptive of life as a mill worker; comic and tragic, defiant and loving. They delight and inspire. "Mill Girls" is a poignant tribute to the mill workers whose hard work brought prosperity and a unique energy to the town where they lived.

- Weaving Musical Threads

Contents

Mill Girls Song

Spinning, weaving , twisting
Hawker, runner, doffer
Spinning, weaving, twisting
Baler, twiner, spooler

Threads through history
sew the Mill girls tae their toon,
Spinners, spoolers, twisters, buddies aw
Gallus needle link of arms
As the Paisley pattern falls
Over generations in an ancient toon

Chorus

Aye the Mill Girls linked their airms,
Coatpins in their hands,
Marched behind a piper through the toon
That foreman turned and fled,
Fae the mocking of the loom,
and the spinning o the Mill Girls patterned on

Chorus

Here's a photograph I've kept,
It's grainy black and white
See the Anchor Mill reflect in grey canal,
No chimney, smoke or wall,
Just a faded idea of
when the Paisley Mill Girls stopped this toon

Chorus

Looking back down,
History's fine thread,
Built on the fingers of these lassies hands
The half time school and the wages small,
the Mill Girls the most radical of all

Chorus

A Streak of Gallus

A streak of gallus ran in
Messages tossed from lips
Mouthed out through the racket
Of machines ratching, clattering
Jarring the nerves to exaggerated speech
Mill lassies mouthy
Crude yet carefully modest
Machines scattering tic tac
Codes from line to line
Menage payments affording
The latest fashion
Then turbans of curlers undone
Arms linked like a Paisley pattern
On their way to the dancing
Threading through streets
Marching, laughing, singing,
Scanning for talent
Gallus lassies, pure dead Gallus

Granny Purcell

At the Ferguslie Mill,
When the horn blew
A sea of girls swarmed
Past Bridge Lane Gatehouse
Flowed down Newton Street.
Granny Purcell waved
From her window
A Mill Girl all her working days

In her gardening years
The factory sent her bobbins
By the sack-full, to throw in the fire
Warm her bones as she sat
Seeing her old workmates'
Laughter sparking in the flames
Her grand-weans played with bobbins
As they watched Mill girls
Stream past Granny's window
In their thousands
Laughter dancing them along
Cramming the streets
Making a whole town stop

Spinning Mill No. 1 at Ferguslie Thread Mill

A middle page spread in the *Architect*
Curtsied to your 'pièce de resistance' style
Brick by brick, 5 storeys
Graced the skyline for 150 years
Before your fine jewels were ripped out
Thrown on rubbish dumps

You were graded, 'A' Listed
To ensure you graced the skyline
For centuries to come
Then left to decay
While greedy builders
Snapped at your heels
Threw matches at your skirts
Moved the pen of the Secretary of State
To condemn you to death
Snapping a thread of history
Your crumbling demise
Eternally playing out on You Tube
History screaming, as you fall

Strike

Five thousand
Marched to Ferguslie calling
Their fellow workmates out
Cat-calling, window breaking
They blockaded the Police
Hat pins stabbing
Fire hoses gushing to keep them
From breaking through the gates
Seventeen days of mayhem
While girls paraded behind a piper
Honking the horns of street cars
Thousands of mocking girls
Followed their manager home
At Paisley Cross they burned his effigy
Ran him out of town yelling
Farewell to Turnbull

The Road to Portobello

As the coach pulled away
She waved to the crowds
Who came to see them off
Sang along to the Mill Girl songs,
On the road to Portobello
A letter yet unopened
burned a hole in her pocket
Three kangaroos across the stamp
her thoughts travelling
to Australia, then moving on
as she counted the many bobbins
that bore her address
On a slip of paper
sealed under colourful thread
wound tight, secretly written
against the rules of work
Now migrating to other countries
America, Mexico, perhaps
the steps of Siberia
Her workmates laughter muted
As she threaded across the world
countryside slipping past her window
She would read the letter later
The letter, she knew
would thread through her days
As she swam in the outdoor pool
Walked the crowded beach
Danced, laughed and sang
The mill far behind them
She would read her letter later
Facing out to sea
Eyes fixed on other lands

Mill Girl Wedding

Whit the mill girls talk aboot
when there's nae men tae hear them.
That's whit a'll miss.

"Whit dae ye dae on yer weddin night? Ye know..."

Not crude, just curious.
Aulder wummin jist smile.

Aye there's been the kiss
that lasted a wee bit too long
when he walked me hame.
He's got us a flat.
A picked the carpet,
blushed at the double bed.
Ma dress-white of course.

Last shift-ma coat whisked away
A' day the banter's a bouncin baw
back an forth, sly and coy,
A' goes too fast.
Tears near when they gift me an iron
drape ma coat roon me
festooned wi ribbons, crepe flowers.

One o the aulder wummin takes me aside
sagely whispers
"Iron the collar and the cuffs first mind."

Cleekin airms work pals sing me hame
carrying a chanty a' salt for good luck.
A' back tae mine for a bit tae eat an drink.
Sittin roon the living room,
mammy, aunties, sisters, pals.

Whit the mill girls talk aboot
when there's nae men tae hear them.

"Don't worry hen, ye'll know whit tae dae."

Bobbin

Wee wooden bobbin hangin'
on a loop of string
roon the door haundle
It's message-
your turn for the stairs.

No jist the peace
of the close dependit on it-
the hale toon's fortunes
spooled roon cotton reels.
Lathe to loom, bobbins spun
a hunner yards of quality cotton,
back when cloth was cut for folk.
Made tae last.

Aye we a' sewed then
mended, dab hauns
at liftin' hems, nippin' in waists,
haudin' the hame the gither.

Wee wooden bobbin,
the machines are silent now.
Fashion's flimsy, cheap.
Luxury flats in refurbished mills
don't need bobbins
on a loop of string.
Naebody takes turns o' the stairs any mair.

May 1904

We're nae dainty ladies
A' peely wally
Slaves tae machines? Aye.
Nimble fingers workin' twine.

A' peely wally
toilin' in swelterin heat.
Nimble fingers workin' twine
for sixty-five pence a week.

Toilin' in swelterin' heat.
Work eat sleep, work eat sleep
for sixty-five pence a week.
Paid less than the men.

Work eat sleep, work eat sleep
Hankwinders, spoolers, whitewinders,
paid less than the men.
Walked oot on the clankin' looms.

Hankwinders, spoolers, whitewinders
A' thoosan mill lassies
walked oot on the clankin' looms.
Defiant. Nae longer!

A thoosan mill lassies,
We're nae dainty ladies.
Defiant. Nae longer!
Slaves tae machines? Naw!

Anchor Mill

At anchor
a titanic red brick ocean liner
every storey studied with long windows.
As a child I counted each pane of glass
superstitiously, in case it sailed off
into the dusk,
surprising pigeons into flight.

Time flowed faster than the river
half moating its base.
The mill has gracefully given into
luxury flats, ergonomically designed offices.
JCBs ripped down a flotilla of out-buildings.

Now I see it
for the first time in years.
Sunlight glows on restored glass.
No time to count window panes.
I know it will always be here.
Preserved-not allowed to sink
into mere rubble?

What the Mill Remembers

The map of me-
men pore and measure.
Spread over gleaming mahogany

Being built
red brick and mortar.
Everyone came to see.

Boilers burn.
Water sings in my pipes
fuelling my vast heart.

Bells ring.
Thousands birthed through my doors
Six till two-two till ten.

Machines mute.
Pigeons croon, rats dart
round my dusty creaking limbo.

Footsteps echo
through my derelict floors.
Men in suits and hard hats.

Computers hum
Zen like in my head.
Telephone voices buzz

Tinny music pounds
a mechanised beat.
A gym in my basement.

People pass
to and fro so quietly.
Carpets muffle their feet.

Gwen McKerrell

Days Out (First Saturday in July)

A caravan of coaches
Cotton Street to Bridge Street
41 in total
all this for us?
We're celebrating a victory
weavers against manufacturers
and in this town
we all know who won
"Sma Shot Day"
Most of Paisley must have turned up
to see us off
tripping over each other
in our Sunday best
taking the scenic route to Braemar
Cheered by the crowd
like we're royalty
and today we really are
The Megaphone heralds our arrival
through Glasgow and the towns
"Good Morning. This is the Paisley Mill girls'
excursion to Braemar on Sma' Shot Day"!
Folks we don't know
smile as we pass
we all wave back
like real VIPs
We don't stop talking
excited chatter
looking at the scenery
as we head north

"Looks just like the postcards"
some of us say
A cup of tea at Stirling
before scrambling back onboard
to Perth for lunch
So many of us
it takes three hotels
to feed us all
very posh
We've only an hour
before boarding again
but we don't complain
Old Scone, Blairgowrie, Glen Shee
We all hold our breath
at Devil's Elbow.
High tea at Crieff
surrounded by pipers
Some of the girls miss the bus
got a bit carried away
A quick cuppa at Stirling
then off again
the homeward stretch
back to Paisley
What a day
still laughing and talking
as we disembark
Paisley folk back out to meet us
'Cos we're special
We're the Mill girls

Diana Dors

She shimmies along Glasgow Road
Her lips kiss the air
a little Diana Dors here and there
Her heels give her a wiggle
plucked eyebrows
black kohl up the back of her legs
doesn't care who sees
A saved hard for black raincoat
(mother takes most of her wages)
you can see the gold inside
She'll be the swell in curlers under a turban
Ready for the Dancin'
She's had her eye on Jimmy Brown
he'll be there
After the Mill

At 14 she'd been swung up at the gates
(Her own mother had started at 12)
Well she was old enough
to start bringing in the money
never did her mother any harm
It's a Company town, a mill town
it's what's expected
They checked her hair for lice, knickers for fleas
and she was in

She's a toe typist
tap tap tapping
spools clattering on shelves
roaring the hit parade
to the rhythm of the machines

as you crouched between them
barefoot, avoiding rats, beetles and machine belts
whipping at your arms
choking on dust, lint and heat
They give you a pound and tuppence
but it's a better wage than the office girls get
despite what they say about the mill girls
but that's only jealousy

She gets on well with the other girls
not The Mistress.
she's scared of her
dreams of home time
when the girls link arms
stream through the gates
no one better get in the way then
The town will be lively
the cinema, the dancin' of course
and she's still thinking about Jimmy Brown

Mindings

D'ye mind the 'lectric?
One of the first places in Paisley
to have electric
was our mill

D'ye mind the recreation club?
the three legged and the sack
They filmed opening day
showed it at The Paisley Palace
We clapped and cheered
as we watched
Jeannie tied up in that sack
falling over her own big feet

D'ye mind the strikes?
In 1907, wilder than us those girls
The stories about Turnbull, the manager
being run out of town
They even stole his doormat

D'ye mind the toe typing?
Aye, I mind when I used to have a big toe
when I worked among rats
and gaffers who didn't treat us
with any more respect
than the rats

D'ye mind the laughs?
The backchat, the friendships
to last a lifetime
gallus lassies
No Fools us

D'ye mind the ciggys, rollers, chocolate?
smuggled into the mill
in Annie's drawers
The pictures after work
and mill trips with us girls

D'ye mind April 1993?
Last mill girl clocked off
and the mill now?
luxury flats!
Would you credit it?
       D'ye mind?

The London

Head down the lavvy pan
well, she said she wanted waves
no washbasins here
you need water for waves
finger waves
beautiful S shapes
curled down her cheek
like Norma Shearer
in The Divorcee
just out at the pictures

Six in a cubicle
legs up against the wall
leaving only two feet
showing at the door.
It's share and share alike
Last week she'd pierced Minnie's ears
two cubicles along
hands trembling
as she held the needle
nervous, but she didn't let on.

The London
The Lavvies
They come here most days
for the banter
the gossip
the one about Maisie and Jim
will they, won't they.

Jenny read the leaves
and told us they would
but we didn't believe her
until we wrapped Maisie's coat in crepe
and clattered saucepan lids down the street
dancing her to married life.

The London is escape
taking us away
from The Mistress
petty rules
deference
freedom, for a short while
The best memories
Keeps us going
as we trail back to the machines

The Real Mill Girls

We built this toon, we did,
with hauns bleedin' and toes achin'
withoot our toil they'd be nae fancy buildins
nae Toon Hall, nae Museum, nae Library
Yon city faithers talk aboot the Clark and Coats Legacy
but it's oor legacy
We did the work
And provided the wealth
Geid yon high heid yins their mansions and power.
Although, these days, wha's left?

Ah remember the day the Finishing Mill
was re-opened by yon Charles & Camilla
Redeveloped – nae mair mills
Aw new fancy hooses for the wealthy
Ah wonder if they ever thocht of us girls
Toilin' awa inside these places
building Paisley Brick by Brick
Nae fancy hooses for us.

Naw, we remember the way it was
So will ye remember the Girls,
now the mansions are gone
the mills replaced?
Will our stories remain
in the fabric of this toon
in your Paisley pattern scarf
and your wee bit bobbin o' threid?

Open the Gates

Here they come, the tides of girls. Arms cleeked
and through the gates: another day. Machine rattle,
run of the mill, the constant drill. Belts grinding,
toes treading, skin and sinew, perpetual motion:
top and drop – piece work – there's a rhythm to it;
switch, twist, twine, doff. And the heat, the slick
hissing hide of the beast as it sweats and shakes. Send
wee Jean for a bucket of steam, and June needs a headless
broom, and Annie's getting married soon. See
her off in a tissue-covered coat, because you've got to laugh:
every morning waiting for the wee red eye to blink
'time'; and at tea breaks, the foreman's beady black eye timing
your wee (he never did work out how one pair
of legs under a lavvy door becomes four).
Well, doff your hat to the girls. Belts grinding, toes
treading, barefoot as vestals, singing above the thunder.
And when the hooter sounds: oh, mill girls, the swagger!
Arms cleeked, belts tight, collars high,
coats gold-lined, surging up Neilston, down Causeyside,
constellations pouring along Mill Street, Thread Street,
Cotton, Gauze. They throw their scarves and toss their hair
in the wind. Tonight they'll dance: spinning, weaving, twisting
till the last girl clocks off, till the shattered flats empty
and the floors collapse. The final song fading in the air
like a thread waiting for history's needle.

Job Descriptions

Ye cuid be a bogie girl wae a cairt fu o reels
A spinner, scissors danglin fae yer finger
A bare-footed twiner, a big toe typist
Staunin aw day, machines twistin away

Ye cuid be a spooler, wrappin an labellin
A repairer, chucking oot the bad
A box shop bender, a baler bandin
The roon ba's wae an Anchor Mills sash

Ye cuid be the family's only earner, Faither deid in the Great War

Ye cuid be a desk girl, a chronicler
A piece worker, ay tryin tae get in front o yersel
A doffer, a shorts girl, a trainer prim an proper
Ye cuid dance in the corridor wae hat an gloves

Ye cuid fa in love

Ye cuid be a ticketer, soor taste o gum oan yer tongue
A gasser, burnin the frays wae a flame
A twister: when the belts snapped like whips ye ran
Yer life in yer hands

Ye cuid sing o'er the thunner

Ye cuid see the Prince o Wales (a wee man caked in make up)
Ye cuid watch the bombs fa oan
Renfrew as ye walked tae work
Ye cuid be a tester, a ball carrier, a runner, a helper

Ye wur never a stranger

Ye cuid curl yer hair, six tae a loo, fur Friday night at La Scala
Get yer ears pierced wae a needle an a cake o soap
Go oan trips tae Saltcoats, Largs, Portobello, Braemar
Ye cuid be wheeled roon the mill oan a bogie cairt

But ye cuidnae work if ye wur mairrit

Ye cuid make friends ye'd never lose
Ye cuid earn the best wages in toon
Ye cuid be the first in yer class tae get a pension
Ye cuid be independent

Ye cuid come hame wae yer fingers red an sair
Ye cuid wake up wae a wad o cotton in yer throat
Ye cuid huv baith yer big toes amputated
Ye cuid look oot sternly fae black an white pictures

Ye cuid be a poem

FERGUSLIE MAXWELLTON SCHOOL, PAISLEY.

Half Timers' School

A rod of light illuminates the cracked
geometry of brick and empty sky.
Here philanthropy at its best, no lack
of stateliness; the master's sculpted eye
saw half an education was better
than none. Hard won hours at low wooden desks
traded factory stour for drills and letters.
Repeat after me, the slow rote of tasks:
half of one is? Half, chorused the small tongues,
hands neatly folded. Who pays attention
now? Heat-scarred, blackened, dumb,
one of five pillars stands amidst the pyre:
present, correct, like a good intention
that refuses to be silenced by fire.

The Rioters

At first glance,
they could pass for elegance:
ladies in Edwardian lace,
hair combed like Venus.

The photograph is stained
with age, but look closer:
this one has hands on her hips,
the others, bare feet
and lassos of twine.

Notice the big toes,
how they turn at an angle,
misshapen, ugly,
seeking the light.

Distorted smiles, distorted feet:
these were the Big Toe Typists,
swollen joints
constantly working,
controlling the speed
of the twisting machines.

Try it yourself:
flex the big toe
up down up down.
Keep moving hour
after hour, shift
after shift.

It makes sense now:
the business-like faces,
leg of mutton sleeves
rolled up, ready for it.

Was it these same ladies
who yelled 'Strike!'
rushed the factory gates,
hissing under fire hoses,
haring through streets,
honking horns.

Wild swans,
they hijacked a tramcar,
turned their stern-faced,
bowler-hatted manager
from his own front door,
dragged his effigy
to the Cross and
danced around
its burnt remains.

Oh ladies, do your toes still ache?

Sonnet for Anchor Mills

In a corner of the car park it lies broken,
Snapped at the waist, wreath of laurels stolen;
The old tattoo obscured by time and moss,
Forgotten and neglected. Such a loss
Of dignity. I wonder what they'd say,
The thousands who at break and fall of day
Passed by the emblem of their labour's pains,
And now to see the sad and crude remains.
For though its heart was always made of stone,
Grown black with smoke, and stamped on iron bone,
Though philanthropic gestures are debated -
To let its memory crack without a sound,
This broken anchor that keeps nothing weighted,
Without a ship to stay, has run aground.

Inheritance

They stand on the bridge
six deep, half hidden
behind the black mass of their skirts.
Tight oval faces caught end-of-shift,
eyes curious, turned towards
the unseen camera.

Back then it was new:
the mill womb cold and cruel,
the bridge functional
as grey industry's cervix,
spilling its dark blood,
killing miracles no saint could fix.

A century of feet crossed its neck,
midwives tending the fire,
the threads of wedding hems
and babies' vests, of empty pockets
and winter blankets, hearts
pushed through the eye of a needle.

Here is our kingdom: Morrisons and petrol.
What would they say, those women
who broke their fingers for our wealth?
Let them speak from their dead dark caves;
lower the bridge
so they may feast their eyes, bright as fish,
on the new millennium,
its well stacked shelves,
silent and deadly
as a spoiled child.

The Bridge

Each week
I awaited its arrival
by the old mill
as I would
a familiar friend

For so long
there was only
smashed windows
and half ruined stone
the silence of
a buried age

Until the bridge
resurrected
like an old saint's
iron bones

does metal hold memory in its core,
does it know water, feel a river's curve?

Here it stands
a graceful ceremony
the load lighter
girded arms
the colour of setting sun

And here I am
on history's back
my feet above water
little flakes of iron
in my blood

The Real Mill Girls

We ken whit it smelled like, aw they miles o threid,
enough tae spool the warld. We mind o the heat,
the machines that made ye deif, the never endin piecework.
We can tell ye aboot yon supervisor, a right bitch,
wha tried tae catch ye smokin in the Londons.
We can tell ye wha wis winchin wha, how this wan
thought she wis the bees knees, an this wan hud a mooth
like a cludgie. We mind o Peter Coats, his lang siller hair,
how the managers sneeviled efter him tae open the door.
We ken how mony hours, how mony fingers twistin threid
it took tae build this toon. Whit'll ye dae when we're aw awa'
an aw that's left is the stanes, an the statues staunin in the rain?
Then, no even that. Cos we're the real mill girls, we wrote the sang –
waeoot us, it's aw jist wurds.

List of Illustrations

Acknowledgements

The Mill Girl Poets would like to acknowledge the assistance of the Paisley Thread Mill Museum: the late Eleanor McAlpine and the late Ellen Farmer MBE, who supported the project from its initial event at the Weaving Musical Threads festival in March 2012; and to Janet Robinson and Margaret Burleigh for their continued support and advice (www. paisleythreadmill.co.uk). We'd also like to acknowledge Evelyn Hood, whose book *Mill Memories* provides timeless stories and anecdotes as heard through the voices of the people who lived and breathed life in the thread mills; and Ajay Close for 'Run of the Mill – Paisley's Mill Lassies' (March 18, 2000), *The Scotsman* (www.ajayclose.co.uk/journalism/ paisleymills.html). Acknowledgements also to Wullie Purcell from Read Raw Ltd (www.readrawltd.co.uk), to the Local Area Committees who have supported this anthology, and last, but definitely not least, to Weaving Musical Threads (www.weavingmusicalthreads.com) for believing in the project, and for the burning of much midnight oil.

- Tracy Patrick on behalf of the *Mill Girls*

I would like to thank my fellow Mill Girl poets for their belief in my work, as well as friends and writers Wullie Purcell, George Walker and Ian Hunter. Without all of you, I doubt that I would muster the confidence to write and further perform my poetry. - Mo Blake

I would like to thank Tony for being a rock, Jack, Mina and Finn Daly for being the best kids ever and in memory of my mum Maureen a former mill girl. - Kathryn Daly

When I was first asked to become part of this project I had no idea that it would take us on the journey it has, and for that I must thank Weaving Musical Threads for the support and opportunity to explore the lives of the mill girls of Paisley through poetry and music. I have found the process both interesting and humbling in the context of providing an insight into the lives of these women, a life which was undoubtedly hard but which they got through with cheerfulness and determination, making lifetime friends along the way. I hope that this anthology gives the reader a useful snapshot of their lives and is as enjoyable to them as it was to us in putting it together. - Gwen McKerrell

Biographies

Mo Blake is one of four directors of Read Raw Ltd (www.readrawltd.co.uk), a group of writers who actively promote writers in Scotland and further afield. Her poetry has been published in various collections, not least the Scotia Bar Finalists Anthology 2009, Ink Sweat & Tears and Earth Love Anthology. She has performed poetry before audiences in Glasgow, Paisley, Perth and Dumfries and her poetry collection is due out soon. Mo also writes short stories and is working on an historical thriller.

Kathryn Daly has never taken a gap year in Timbuktu and doesn't speak Mongolian. She has been writing since she was 7 and has been published in anthologies and magazines mostly in Scotland. She won the Craftex 2009 award for Creative Writing. Kathryn is currently writing a novel.

Gwen McKerrell has been writing poems for several years and been published in the Earth Love Anthology. She has performed in a number of venues in Glasgow such as the CCA, Tchai Ovna and at the Mitchell Library as part of the Aye Write Festival. As part of Weaving Musical Threads, Gwen has performed in several venues in Paisley.

Tracy Patrick is an MLitt graduate of Glasgow University. She performs widely, has won poetry slams, had a poem featured on the Glasgow Subway, and had work published in numerous magazines, including *New Writing Scotland 21, Cutting Teeth, Southlight, The Eildon Tree,* www. laurahird. com/showcase/tracypatrick.html and glasgowtosaturn.com/archive. Her play, 'Three Marys,' was performed at the West End Festival. Tracy founded and edited the Earth Love poetry magazine and Anthologies, published in 2013. Tracy is writing her second novel

Anna MacDonald is a musician , singer and songwriter who performs solo and with her trio. She grew up in Glasgow with strong family connections to the Isle of Skye. In 2010 her EP ' You Held Out Your Hand' was released to fantastic reviews. She has played in a number of festivals, including Celtic Connections and to great media acclaim embarked on a UK wide promotional tour during which she supported various artists such as Kathryn Tickell and Paper Aeroplanes. Anna has also performed her own compositions with London's
Portobello Orchestra. 2011 saw the release of her second EP ' Paper Flowers' . Since the beginning of 2013 she has been recording in Sardinia (for her next album!) , playing in LA and Europe.

Mill Girls

A collection of poems remembering and celebrating
the passion and resilience of the women who worked
in the thread mills and the making of a town.

"Whit'll ye dae when we're aw awa',
an aw that's left is the stanes,
an the statues staunin in the rain?
Then, no even that.
Cos we're the real mill girls, we wrote the sang -
waeoot us, it's aw jist WURDS."

ISBN 978 1 907000 13 3

Art
Film
Crafts
Music
Dance
Writing
Theatre
Heritage

WMT
Weaving Musical Threads
A'fighe Snàthainn Ceòlmhòr

9 781907 000133   £5.99

HELEN CRUMMY

WHOM DYKES DIVIDE

A STORY OF THE NIDDRIE COALBEARERS